Original title:
The Mango Sun

Copyright © 2025 Creative Arts Management OÜ
All rights reserved.

Author: Olivia Sterling
ISBN HARDBACK: 978-1-80586-386-1
ISBN PAPERBACK: 978-1-80586-858-3

In Laughter of Golden Weather

In fields of gold, we play and cheer,
With fruits that gleam, we hold them near.
Each bite a giggle, sweet delight,
As sticky juice drips, oh what a sight!

We juggle them high, we toss and roll,
Each plop and splat, a funny goal.
The laughter rings through sunny days,
In squishy mess, we find our ways.

Nature's Sweet Gift of Light

A treasure hangs from branches bold,
Its shiny skin, a sight to behold.
We wear it as hats, oh what a pair,
A fruity fashion show—we laugh and stare!

With scoops of joy, we dig right in,
Our sticky hands, a win-win grin.
In every bite, a chuckle grows,
As friends go wild in sweet, ripe throes.

Sun-Ripened Rituals

Dancing under rays so bright,
We toast to fruits, what a delight!
With slurps and smacks, a silly feast,
Our giggles rise, not for the least!

Each bite conspiratorial, we share a joke,
In juicy circles, we giggle and poke.
Who knew such joy would come from skin,
Of golden orbs, our laughter within?

A Luminescent Harvest

In golden glow, we gather round,
With cheers and laughter, joy unbound.
As fruit flies swirl, our giggles bloom,
In nature's kitchen, there's always room!

With peels like confetti, we revel and play,
Our playground of flavor, hip hip hooray!
From tangy bites to bursts of cheer,
The sweetness brings our hearts so near.

A Harvest of Golden Rays

In the tree, a golden glow,
Fruits hang low, in quite a row.
Squirrels dance with acrobatic flair,
While I stand wishing I had a chair.

Plump and round, they tease my eyes,
With every breeze, a sweet surprise.
They giggle and bounce, oh what a sight,
I'm plotting my snack, it feels so right.

Basking in Juiciness

A bite so sweet, it makes me grin,
Juice dribbles down, oh where to begin?
Pop one in, and the laughter starts,
As I make unexpected fruit-art.

Neighbors peek through their windows wide,
Watching me slip on juice, I slide!
It's a slippery game, but oh so fun,
Welcome to my fruity carnival run!

Summer's Luminous Treasure

Sunshine captured, in nature's treat,
A burst of flavor in summer heat.
Frogs jump high, the laughter flies,
As I munch on slices, oh such blissful ties.

With sweet sticky fingers, I dance around,
Spilling juice like a circus clown.
The neighbors chuckle from their porch seat,
While I'm diving deep in this summer feat.

Ripe Hues of Afternoon

In the afternoon glow, colors collide,
Juicy treasures, I can't hide.
I twirl with delight, wearing a grin,
While sticky hands, my humble kin.

Clouds drift by with a knowing glance,
As I make every bite a funny dance.
Laughing hard, I trip and fall,
Still licking fingers, it's a sweet free-for-all.

Fruitful Embrace of Daybreak

When morning yawns and stretches wide,
A fruit parade begins to glide.
Bananas giggle, apples prance,
As oranges twirl in a sunrise dance.

The squirrel jokes, the mockingbird sings,
While watermelon plays with shiny rings.
Grapes are whispering silly rhymes,
And cherries blush in morning chimes.

Peaches play hopscotch on the dew,
While pineapples tumble, oh what a view!
A jolly feast in the light of day,
With fruity friends in a bright display.

Limes burst out laughing, zest aglow,
While berries tell tales of the night's show.
A fruity embrace, merry and bold,
In this morning's charm, pure joy unfolds.

A Luminous Orchard's Lullaby

In an orchard bright, the breeze does tease,
With apples singing like buzzing bees.
Under the branches, jokes take flight,
As fruits giggle under the soft twilight.

Peaches play tag with a bouncing pear,
While cherries spin in carefree air.
Grapefruits chuckle, rolling about,
As lemons shout, 'We're sweet, no doubt!'

Kiwis tell tales, so juicy and round,
While nuts crack up without a sound.
The nectar flows in hilarious streams,
As the orchard bursts with laughing dreams.

Coconuts sway like they own the place,
While berries blush, lighting up their face.
Each fruit a character, bright and spry,
In this lively orchard, where laughter won't die.

Sunset's Nectar

At dusk, the fruits begin to sigh,
With orange clouds, they wave goodbye.
Melons burst into a rhyming spree,
While grapes start a dance, oh so free.

Currants giggle as they roll down hills,
And strawberries share their sweet little thrills.
Peaches toss jokes in the twilight glow,
While kiwis wear hats with a cheeky bow.

Papayas cheer, their voices soar,
Under the sky, they want more and more.
Bananas run races into the night,
In a fruity frenzy, such a delight!

As twilight hugs the horizon tight,
Nectar flows sweet in the fading light.
Each fruit's a star in the last sunbeam,
Together they laugh, living the dream.

Sunlit Serenade in Paradise

In paradise, where the fruits laugh loud,
Pineapples dance, drawing a crowd.
Mangoes waltz with a zesty flip,
While berries giggle, a tempting trip.

Citrus serenades in the sunny rays,
Whilst guavas toast to joyful days.
Dragonfruit glimmers with whimsy and flair,
As apples spin tales in the warm air.

The picnic unfolds, with smiles galore,
As fruits feast together, never a bore.
Watermelon rolls and nectarines cheer,
In this sunlit scene, joy is near.

With each fruity jest, they twirl and sway,
In a paradise bright, they laugh and play.
A sunny song with a humor so grand,
The happiest fruits in this colorful band.

Vibrant Lullabies of the Tropics

In the fields where laughter grows,
Colorful fruits play hide and pose.
A toe can tap to their sweet beat,
As juices splash on dancing feet.

Beneath the tree, a nap takes flight,
With dreams of snacks both day and night.
A fruit hat placed atop my head,
I chase the giggles as they spread.

Glorious Waves of Sunkissed Color

Waves of flavor crash and swirl,
A nutty dance, a fruity twirl.
With every bite, the world's a stage,
Bright hues spark laughter, we engage.

Sunkissed sweetness in a bowl,
Tickles the funny bone and soul.
Splashing juice from cheek to chin,
Time to dive into this juicy spin.

Cherishing the Sweet Embrace

In a patch of warmth, we twirl and roll,
Sweet nectar lifts the heaviest soul.
With hugs of flavor, we relish each bite,
Sticky fingers make for pure delight.

A playful wink from nature's cheer,
Giggles echo, loud and clear.
Fortunes found where fruit trees sway,
In laughter's realm, we dance and play.

Light's Juicy Portrait

A canvas bright with fruity glee,
Splashes of sunshine dousing me.
With every drip, a story's spun,
Of cheeky fruits in endless fun.

Chasing shadows of the sweet delight,
Where silly faces steal the light.
Brushstrokes of laughter fill the air,
In every bite, joy's art laid bare.

Golden Nectar Horizon

In the sky, a ball of gold,
Makes the stories of fruit unfold.
It blinks and winks, oh such a tease,
And warms up all the buzzing bees.

Children laugh with sticky hands,
Searching for juice in distant lands.
They slip and slide on grassy hills,
While they chase down the fruity thrills.

Embrace of Summer's Glow

A giant smile, so round and bright,
Turns boredom into pure delight.
With splashes loud and giggles sweet,
We dance around in summer heat.

Laughter echoes through the trees,
As we dodge the sticky breeze.
With every slice, we share our glee,
Cheek to cheek, just you and me.

Juices of Midday Fire

A fiery orb, high in the sky,
Turns all the kids into a pie.
With cheeks so full and voices grand,
We giggle, grow, and make a stand.

We spin like tops in fruity bliss,
Caught in happiness, we can't miss.
Sweet nectar drips down on our clothes,
In a mess, our laughter grows.

Sweetness in the Silhouette

Twilight brings a golden hue,
Shapes and shadows dance anew.
With every bite, the world feels right,
As day turns softly into night.

A sweet surprise in every drop,
We giggle as we munch and plop.
Sticky fingers and brightened eyes,
Under the twinkle of starry skies.

The Joy of Sun-Kissed Flesh

Jumping in the warmth so bright,
With laughter soaring, taking flight.
Banana peels beneath my feet,
Oops, that's a slippery treat!

Giggles echo, summer's call,
I tumble down, but have a ball.
Sunscreen slathered on my face,
I'm a target in this race!

Belly flops and splashes loud,
We make waves, we make the crowd.
Chasing ice cream on the run,
Fingers sticky, oh so fun!

Chasing shadows, laughter rings,
Underneath the sun we sing.
With friends and fruits, we can't complain,
This golden joy shall be our gain!

Glimmering Currents of Flavor

Beneath the trees, we find delight,
   Sipping nectar, what a sight!
  Fruits and giggles all around,
With each bite, new laughs abound.

Tickled tastes on teasing tongues,
   Juicy tales we've now begun.
  Messy faces, hands like bees,
Here's a bite, oh, have you seen?

Chasing flavors, oh, what fun,
  A treasure map for everyone!
  Lemonade spills, giggles flow,
In this garden, we steal the show!

Juicy dreams thanks to the sun,
Sweet adventures, we have won.
  With each nibble, joy's in sight,
These glimmering bursts are pure delight!

Glowing Reflections of Nature

Reflecting shimmer on my skin,
Wiggly worms think they can win!
While we dance on blades of grass,
Sneaky ants just want to pass.

Nature's laughter in the breeze,
Chasing shadows, oh, with ease.
Frogs that leap and birds that sing,
Bring forth joy in everything!

Bright petals covering the ground,
Where silly moments can be found.
A butterfly steals my hat,
Oh no, come back! You silly brat!

The sun is shining, laughter's near,
With every giggle, have no fear.
This juicy life, so full of cheer,
Brings glows of laughter throughout the year!

A Tapestry of Golden Light

In golden threads, we weave our day,
With silly hats and games to play.
Each little giggle a shining strand,
Spinning tales across the land.

Leaping forward, silly sings,
With dandelions, we make wings.
Chasing sunbeams, down we roll,
In this glee, we find our soul!

Potato salad on my face,
Guess it's time to win this race!
Kicking back in pure delight,
What a charming, sunny sight!

Our laughter echoes in the air,
A tapestry that we all share.
With every joke, with every sight,
We celebrate this golden light!

A Symphony of Summer's Bounty

In the grove, fruit dangles low,
Sticky fingers, oh what a show!
Laughter echoes, give it a try,
Juicy bites make taste buds fly.

Swatting flies with a mango slice,
Each plop on the ground is rather nice.
Messy faces, what a delight,
Sunshine smiles, it feels so right.

Friends gather, a fruity parade,
Salsa dancing under the shade.
Wobbly chairs, laughter spills,
Sipping juice gives such sweet thrills.

Endless chatter fills the air,
Sticky joy is everywhere.
A symphony of flavors bold,
In these moments, our hearts unfold.

Sunlit Euphoria of Every Season

Bubbles rise from fizzy treats,
Margarita madness, what fun it creates!
Sun shines brighter, laughter's loud,
Joyful chaos, a festing crowd.

Flip-flops flop, a dance of glee,
Fruits and friends, wild as can be!
With sticky hands and playful flair,
We guzzle snacks without a care.

Tropic breezes bring cheeky grins,
Slippers slide, oh the spinning spins!
Giggles burst with every splash,
Life's a party, a vibrant clash.

Seasons change, but fun remains,
Fruitful laughter like sugar canes.
Every moment a juicy find,
Together, we're forever twined.

Golden Tropic Dream

In a backyard, shade is bliss,
Sipping drinks, can't resist!
Bumbling bees buzz around cheer,
No worries here, just joy and beer.

Lime and zest on summer's breath,
Silly laughs, we conquer stress.
Quick-footed snacks race on the plate,
Watch your toes, don't be late!

Sunkissed faces, a playful tease,
Tropical vibes bring down the knees.
We toss the fruit, it flies high,
Dodge and giggle, oh my, oh my!

Clinking glasses, tales unfurl,
In this dream, we dance and twirl.
Golden gleams on every side,
Wild as the waves, we're full of pride.

Radiance of Citrus Bliss

Citrus slices, colors parade,
Every bite's a sweet upgrade.
Sour faces in the sun's warm light,
Love these fruits that take a bite!

Juicy dribbles paint our clothes,
Sticky hugs from where fun flows.
Squeezed lemon on the tongue,
Even grumpy folks feel young!

Juggling oranges, careful now,
Up in the air, take a bow!
Laughter rings through summer's haze,
Citrus joy, it's our phase!

We sip and chat till stars appear,
Magic moments, loud and clear.
Radiance brightens every layer,
Fruits and friends, forever savior.

A Tidal Wave of Radiance

A fruit rolls down the street,
Orange and yellow, quite a feat.
Chasing it feels like a race,
Running in a comical space.

Shiny skin and a big grin,
It bounces back, let the fun begin.
I trip and giggle as it lands,
In the hands of mischievous bands.

Splash of juice on my new shirt,
A sticky mess, my dessert's flirt.
Each bite brings laughter, what a scene,
My fruity joy, a sunny dream.

So here's to laughter, sweet and bright,
Under the glow of pure delight.
Join the dance of nature's cheer,
With this fruity friend, we have no fear.

Harvesting the Light of Day

A burst of color in the sky,
I reach to pluck, oh my, oh my!
It pops and bounces, a playful tease,
Rolling around like it's got a breeze.

Gather 'round, let's start the fun,
Harvesting joy beneath the sun.
With each squish, we all erupt,
In laughter, joyfully corrupt.

A juggling act of nature's treat,
Balancing fun on my two feet.
One flies high, another slips,
Juicy landing and silly quips.

In the garden, laughter reaps,
Under the golden, musty heaps.
Join the fun, the bright array,
As we harvest the light of day.

Nature's Harvest of Illuminated Joy

In the orchard, a zesty dance,
Fruits play tag, not a chance.
Orange and yellow, quite a sight,
Nature's giggle in morning light.

Rolling with friends, we can't stop,
A fruit parade, it's quite the hop.
Splashes of juice, a vibrant spree,
Each bite a morsel of glee.

With every chomp, a silly tune,
The sunbeams sing, the cows go 'moo!'
We laugh until our bellies ache,
In the warmth of a fruity wake.

So gather round this joyful feast,
Nature's bounty, to say the least.
With hearts aglow, let spirits play,
Harvesting joy in a funny way.

Warm Glow of Seasonal Dreams

The glow is bright, we twirl and spin,
Dancing around as we all grin.
A fruity dream under the trees,
Where laughter floats upon the breeze.

Bouncing fruits like a game of catch,
Each wobbly move, a perfect match.
With every giggle, the fun expands,
Comedic chaos, oh, how it stands!

Splattered smiles and sticky hugs,
Rolling fruit and wiggly bugs.
In this glow of joyous beams,
We dance our way through seasonal dreams.

So take a bite, let laughter bloom,
With every nibble, erase the gloom.
In this sunny, silly scene,
We'll savor life, forever keen.

Melodies of Citrus Gold

In a grove where laughter grows,
A fruit plays peek-a-boo,
It swings in silly breezes,
Like a child with gum on shoes.

Sweet whispers fill the air,
With every burst of cheer,
Those fruity friends are dancing,
As if they've had too much beer.

Underneath the sun's bold gaze,
They blurt out juicy puns,
Like sour faces at their jokes,
Yet still, they're tasty runs.

So come and join the fun parade,
With laughter, juice, and zest,
In this golden orchard's shade,
Where fruit is always blessed.

Gleam of the Fruitful Dawn

At sunrise, giggles climb the trees,
As fruits perform their morning plays,
They juggle seeds like tiny bees,
And laugh in their fruity ways.

The branches sway in pure delight,
As citrus sings a silly song,
An orange slips and takes a flight,
And bounces back where it belongs.

With vibrant hues upon the floor,
The fruit's a bit too bold,
They share their tales of life and lore,
As if the day's been told.

So let us raise a glass or two,
To mornings bright and free,
Where every hue is just like you,
And laughter's the best spree!

Harvesting Light from the Sky

When dusk descends with fruity cheer,
A couple of peaches start to dance,
They laugh away their daily fear,
And invite the stars for a chance.

Each bouncy bounce creates a spark,
As shadows twirl in playful flares,
Pumpkins grin, oh what a lark,
While blueberries form silly chairs.

The harvest time brings glee anew,
As baskets roll on edges bright,
With every fruit both bold and true,
They gather laughter from the light.

So pluck a smile from nature's stash,
With every taste, a silly shove,
In this grand banquet, oh what a bash,
Where joy is served with love!

A Tapestry of Mango Dreams

In a land of dreams where fruits reside,
A twisted tale of sweetness flows,
With tango moves and wobbly slides,
Where every fruit in laughter glows.

Bananas slide like they're on ice,
And guavas take a funny spin,
Each chuckle adds a cat's meow slice,
As they relay their stories in gin.

With mango wishes and berry schemes,
They craft a world of wobbly cheer,
A tapestry woven with fruity beams,
Where humor's found in every sphere.

So join this banquet, take a seat,
With giggles served and joy adorned,
For in this grove, life is sweet,
And laughter's never scorned.

Cornucopia of Glimmering Tints

In the orchard laughter grows,
Bananas take dance on their toes.
Peaches wear shoes made of cream,
While plums jump high, it's a fruity dream.

Papayas throw parties, quite a bash,
Mangoes play tag, they're sly and brash.
A grape giggles, falls in a heap,
The fruit parade's a riot; no sleep!

Berries sing tunes from a berry band,
Pineapples sway, looking quite grand.
Lemons juggle limes with flair,
Such antics make all fruits unaware!

As sunlight gleams, the fruits say 'cheers!'
With fruity punchlines, they ease our fears.
In this orchard of whimsy, all take flight,
Each bite's a giggle, oh what a sight!

Gentle Flicker of Citrus Flavors

Citrus zests in a cheeky race,
Oranges wink with a cheeky face.
Lemons toss laughs like confetti,
While limes roll giggles, feeling quite petty.

Grapefruits try to steal the show,
But tangerines put on quite the glow.
They skip and hop in a citrus sway,
Chasing each other 'til the end of the day.

Mandarins dance in a flavorsome dance,
Each juicy bite gives a fruity chance.
Jokes fly high, like seeds on the breeze,
Sun-kissed laughter, just like sunshine leaves!

Citrus lemons sing in delightful croon,
While oranges plot under the moon.
In this citrus soup, we can't help but laugh,
With a squeeze of joy, it's a zesty path!

An Odyssey in Warm Hues

Golden glimmers in a fruity land,
Fruits wearing crowns, oh isn't it grand?
Peaches in sunglasses, quite a scene,
While nectarines twirl in a shimmer of cream.

Cherries swing high from their leafy throne,
While kiwis practice their best zany groan.
Bananas orchestrate the harvest's cheer,
And berries giggle, rotating with flair!

Pineapples spin with a crown fit to wear,
While melons play catch in the sunlight's glare.
Mirth fills the air in this vibrant spree,
As each fruit shares a silly decree!

Under the sky, their colors unite,
An odyssey of flavors, pure delight.
Every crunch brings a chorus, a song,
In this tapestry of laughter, we all belong!

Sun-Spun Delight Unraveled

Whimsical waves of yellow and gold,
Fruits telling tales, both funny and bold.
A pumpkin chuckles as squash cracks a grin,
In the sun's warm glow, the laughter begins.

Berries bounce, as if jumping on air,
While giggly melons toss banter to share.
The stalks sway gently, giving a cheer,
As veggies join in, saying, "Let's persevere!"

Glorious hues wrap around in a swirl,
Each fruit spins stories, letting joy unfurl.
Through the laughter and jests, our hearts find their place,

In the sunlight's embrace, we all find our space!

So, pull up a chair and join in the fun,
In this sun-spun realm, we all are as one.
With humor and cheer, we'll gather around,
Where fruits and veggies wear joy like a crown!

Daydreams in Citrus Shades

In a land of yellow bliss,
I tripped on a citrus twist.
Laughter danced between the trees,
Who knew fruit could tease with ease?

A squirrel wore a fruit hat bold,
Claiming riches in ripe gold.
I asked him for a sweet delight,
He winked and vanished out of sight.

Banana peels caused quite a scene,
Where slipping leads to juicy dreams.
Grapefruit tossed me a cheeky grin,
At this rate, I'll be his twin!

So here I sit, with zest in hand,
Creating chaos in fruitland.
A daydream gone terribly wrong,
Yet in my heart, I hum a song.

The Taste of Warm Embrace

A fruit parade upon my plate,
It greets me like a warm soulmate.
With every bite, a giggle bursts,
Juicy sweetness, oh, it quirts!

The silly drips and sticky mess,
Decorate my summer dress.
Friends all laugh as juice does flow,
We're merry in this vibrant show.

Sipping smoothies, feel the cheer,
Fruits are marching, loud and clear.
A pineapple with shades on tight,
Declared it's ready for the night!

In this warmth, we share our tales,
Of fruity mishaps and wild fails.
With every bite, we come alive,
Making memories, we all thrive.

Elegy for a Summer Glow

Oh, summer fruit, where did you go?
You rolled away, now I feel low.
Your vibrant hues, a fleeting sight,
Now I'm left with snackless nights.

An orange danced upon my floor,
Promised me there'd be much more.
But off it rolled, a jester's glee,
Leaving me with just a spree.

I mourn the taste of sweet delight,
Like lost dreams in the fading light.
Watermelons weep for their kin,
Meanwhile, I search for where to begin.

Yet hope remains, when seasons change,
New fruits will come, it feels so strange.
So here I sit, with bittersweet cheer,
Ready to laugh, though missed you dear.

Light Ripening with Colors

Colors popping all around,
In this fruity playground found.
Cherries giggle, oranges tease,
While grapes hang low, swaying with ease.

The laughing lemon takes the lead,
Telling jokes to all in need.
With zesty puns that never stop,
A comedy show on every crop!

Avocados, shy, they hide away,
Until they're smashed in quite the fray.
Guac on chips is quite the skill,
Each crunchy bite is such a thrill.

So join the fun, don't be afraid,
In this bright fruit parade we've made.
With every joke and tasty bite,
We savor joy and pure delight.

Waves of Sweetness and Warmth

In the beachside hut, there's a fruit parade,
Chasing down a snack that can't dissuade.
Such juicy danger in every bite,
Laughter spills out, what a silly sight!

With each squish and drip, the antics grow,
Slipping on peels, putting on a show.
A sticky mess, we'll wear it proud,
Amidst our giggles, oh so loud!

Bright colors gleaming under the sky,
Who needs a plan when fruit flies by?
Swatting bugs like a comedic dance,
Moments like these, we seize our chance!

Silly shouts while we share a taste,
Not one drop of joy will go to waste.
From laughter and fruit, we can't refrain,
A sun-kissed life—a sweet, silly gain!

The Dance of Tropic Blessings

Twirling like dancers, we take our chance,
With fruit in hand, we begin to prance.
Under gleeful skies, let chaos reign,
As sticky fingers cause delightful pain!

A fruit bowl tumbles—it's quite a sight,
Rolling and bouncing, what sheer delight!
We dive and dodge, on a wild spree,
Chasing down snacks, oh, what glee!

Each juicy morsel is a clever tease,
The squeeze leads to giggles, oh, how it frees!
With faces bright and laughter high,
We dance in bliss, just you and I!

Who knew that bites could spark such joy?
A tropical mess, oh my, oh boy!
The sun may shine, but we hold the fun,
With every chuckle, our hearts have won!

Rays of Radiance on Fruitful Shores

Glimmers of gold on a juicy sphere,
We gather around, fueled by cheer.
In the warmth of light, our spirits soar,
Each slice reveals laughter galore!

Rolling in laughter, shared delight,
With juicy splashes, what a sight!
Fruits fly through the air with grace,
Landing in bowls, oh, the perfect place!

Faces shimmering with a sticky grin,
Smiling as friends join in on the din.
With every bite, our worries dissolve,
In a fruity frenzy, we all evolve!

A festival of flavors, what a delight,
Under rays that make even shadows bright.
Let's play the fool and raise a cheer,
For every bite brings us near!

Exotic Echoes in the Breeze

Whispers of laughter float on the air,
As fruits call us like they really care.
Bouncing through shadows, we make our way,
Toward the playground of fruity play!

Each curvy slice brings a joyful sound,
The crunch of delight spreads abound.
A catapult of flavors, we all might slip,
Grinning as we take another trip!

Juggling the fruits, what a mad feat,
With comedy gold in every sweet treat!
Baskets overflow as smiles do too,
Silly and sweet, just me and you!

In the golden glow, we share the joy,
Who needs fancy toys when fruits deploy?
Chasing echoes through the fragrant breeze,
Laughter and sweetness bring us to our knees!

Echoes of a Solstice Fruit

In a tree, so high and bright,
A fruit with laughter takes its flight.
It giggles as it swings with grace,
A golden smile upon its face.

Dropping down, it rolls away,
It trips on leaves, and oh, the sway!
A dance of flavors, sweet and wild,
Reminds us all of blissful child.

Who knew a fruit could be so fun?
The summer's prankster, on the run!
With juice that sprays, it gives a wink,
And makes us laugh, more than we think.

So grab a slice, let's have a bite,
In sunny glow, our hearts feel light.
With every taste, the giggles rise,
Echoes of joy beneath bright skies.

The Dancer Beneath the Palm

Beneath the palm, a party starts,
A fruit's serenade for beating hearts.
It shimmies left and then to right,
With zestful moves, oh what a sight!

It twirls and spins with tape and flair,
All the while, without a care.
Passersby chuckle, join the spree,
As tropical rhythms set them free.

In a twist! It lands, oh what a mess,
Covered in grass, a fruity dress.
Laughter erupts from all around,
This silly dance is quite renowned!

Now gather 'round, there's more to share,
A fruity show, sensational fare.
One last twirl, then it's time to munch,
The giggly delight, our perfect lunch.

Sunlit Orchard's Gentle Kiss

In an orchard, joyfully laid,
Where sunlight plays and trickery's made.
A round delight with a cheeky grin,
Invites you in for a sugary spin.

With every bite, it plays a song,
A chorus sweet that can't be wrong.
In sticky hands, we share the cheer,
As giggles bubble, oh so clear.

How did it roll? Did it just fly?
We ponder as it makes us sigh.
Its slyness brightens the summer's day,
A sweet surprise that leads us to play.

So let's embrace this sunny bliss,
Wrapped in laughter, we reminisce.
A dance of flavors in every taste,
In this orchard, not a moment waste.

Golden Essence in Vivid Skies

Above the field, a treasure gleams,
Reflecting sunlight in golden beams.
It sways and hops, a bouncing ball,
This fruit seems ready for a fall.

With every drop, it makes a splash,
Causing giggles in a merry dash.
It rolls like laughter, bright and bold,
A story of mischief yet untold.

A serious fruit? Quite the debate!
For every bite, a twist of fate.
It flips and flops, then starts to tease,
Chasing raindrops in the balmy breeze.

So gather 'round, let's share the fun,
With every taste, it's just begun.
In vivid skies, where smiles are free,
This golden joy brings harmony.

Essence of Evening Glow

A fruit with a smile, oh what a sight,
Sticky fingers dancing with pure delight.
It rolls off the table, oh what a mess,
Down the dog's back, it's an evening dress.

The laughter erupts like bubbles in champagne,
As we chase it around, like it's playing a game.
What joy it brings, a tasty, sweet jest,
In the circus of dinner, it's simply the best.

Hues of Warmth Unfurled

Bright orange blushes, with a wink and a grin,
As kids make a splatter that leads to a win.
With faces adorned in a sticky embrace,
Who knew that dessert could be such a race?

Be careful, dear friend, as you take that big bite,
For juice may escape, oh what a fright!
But laughter erupts, as we all start to play,
In this fruity adventure, we find our own way.

Juicy Echoes of a Golden Day

In the shade of the tree, we gather around,
With giggles and jokes, oh what lovely sounds.
A slice of pure sunshine, dribbles cascade,
As we slip on the peel, oh what a charade!

Each bite is a burst, like laughter in spring,
The juice on our shirts, what joy it can bring.
A fruit-flavored frenzy, with games that we play,
It's a sticky sweet dance at the end of the day.

Shimmers of Sun-Drenched Bliss

With shades of delight, we savor the fun,
As one brave soul tries to juggle just one.
It bounces and wobbles, oh dear what a sight,
As we burst into giggles, all under the light.

We squeal with delight at the mess we have made,
With laughter that echoes, oh sweet escapade!
As we wipe off the juice with a grin on our face,
This joyous adventure, a sticky embrace.

Days Painted in Golden Liquid

A fruit that glows, oh what a sight,
Dripping juice, a pure delight.
On cheeks and chins, it makes a mess,
Sticky fingers, who would guess?

Swinging limbs, they sway with glee,
As laughter dances wild and free.
Underneath the tree, we plot and scheme,
To snag the last bite, it's a team dream!

Juices flying with every bite,
As we munch and giggle, pure delight.
A juicy crown, we wear it proud,
With laughter booming, oh so loud!

Endless summer, sweet and bliss,
Let's indulge, we cannot miss.
Golden nectar, sunlit fun,
In this feast, we've surely won!

Whispers of a Tropical Dawn

Morning calls with a citrus cheer,
Golden drop dreams, oh so near.
With sleepy eyes, we awake in bliss,
Fruit on the table, who could resist?

The parrot squawks, "Eat your treat!"
As we gobble up the golden sweet.
Sticky giggles fill the air,
With every slice, we dance and flare.

Bright hues splash across the plate,
Belly laugh, as we anticipate.
A feast of fruit, for every hand,
Chasing flavors, oh so grand!

With each bite, we claim our throne,
Juicy crowns, we've truly grown.
With funny faces, we strike a pose,
In the morning glow, anything goes!

Citrus Gold Beneath the Canopy

Under leafy shade, we feast so bright,
Round and plump, a fruity sight.
With giggles shared, we take a bite,
Juicy goodness makes the day just right.

Roll the fruit, it's quite a game,
Sticky laughter, we'll stake our claim.
With silly faces, we take a chance,
In juicy puddles, we laugh and dance.

The sun peeks in, joins the fun,
A zesty burst, our race has begun.
Who can eat the most today,
With silly hats, we laugh and play!

Covered in gold, we're quite the sight,
Belly laughs in pure delight.
In this shade, our giggles hum,
What a silly, sunny kingdom!

Symphony of Bright Refreshment

A bowl so bright, it steals the show,
Golden jewels lined in a row.
With every bite, the laughter flows,
As juice spills forth like a comical show!

Silly faces, we try to contain,
As sweet juice drips down, a sticky chain.
Giggle fits take over the day,
In our silly fruit parade, hooray!

With juicy pops, we serenade,
Each bite a note, a grand charade.
Who knew fruit could bring such glee,
As we dance and splash, wild and free!

Laughter echoes in the sunny space,
Who knew breakfast could be a race?
With each sweet bite, the fun is spun,
A fruity symphony, oh what fun!

Twilight's Glow in Fruity Abundance

In twilight's gleam, a fruity dance,
With every bite, a juicy chance.
The laughter flows, oh what a sight,
As friends devour, pure delight.

Beneath the tree with leaves so wide,
A sweet surprise, we laugh and chide.
The fruit parade, a merry crew,
With sticky hands and faces too.

Flavor bursts, a silly game,
The sticky treasure, none to blame.
We juggle fruits, a wacky race,
A fruity battlefield, oh what a place!

As twilight fades, we dance with glee,
A fruity feast, just you and me.
The night may fall, but smiles remain,
In juicy joy, we'll stake our claim.

Lush Tropics Beckon the Day

Morning sun calls from lowly trees,
A luscious breakfast, oh what tease!
We bounce and hop, it's quite absurd,
The simple fruit, our daily word.

With giggles soft, we take a bite,
The tart and sweet, pure delight.
Our funny faces, oh so bright,
As juice drips down, what a sight!

We toss and share, a fruity fight,
Who knew a snack could feel so right?
With every chew, we joke and grin,
A tropical day, that's where we win!

The lush green calls us out to play,
With laughs and fruits, we welcome the day.
In nature's lap, we find our way,
In fruity fun, come what may!

Whispers of Light in Every Bite

In every slice, a giggle wakes,
As sunshine whispers, laughter shakes.
An orange twist, a melon slide,
Juicy joy, we cannot hide.

We play with flavors, what a mess,
A fruity feast, we must confess.
With silly hats and faces too,
Each yummy crunch, a laugh anew.

Fruits in hand, we strike a pose,
As flies zoom 'round, chaos grows!
Sweet delight, we raise a cheer,
A happy group, our choice is clear!

Beneath the rays, our smiles ignite,
In every bite, we find pure light.
So eat and laugh, do not be shy,
In fruity fun, we all can fly!

Colorful Caress of Sunbeams

In colors bright, we take a stroll,
A feast of fruits, we seize our goal.
With sunbeams shining on our face,
We dive right in, a wild embrace.

Juicy morsels, splashes play,
With every slice, we laugh away.
A pineapple hat? Oh what a sight!
Coconut crowns, pure delight!

We spin and jump in fruity glee,
Each bite a burst, oh can't you see?
With playful puns and silly cheer,
A festival of joy is here!

As colors merge with laughter's flow,
We celebrate the sun's warm glow.
In every bite, a story spun,
With fruits & friends, we have our fun!

A Cornucopia of Luminous Hues

In a bowl of sunshine's grin,
A fruit that wears a golden skin.
It rolls and slips on kitchen floors,
Delighting kids, they squeal and roar.

With every slice, a dance ensues,
As sticky fingers claim their dues.
A fruity feast, we laugh and cheer,
This fruity buddy brings us near.

Its scent, a joke upon the breeze,
A burst of laughter, never leaves.
We toss the seeds, a playful game,
With each small splash, we shout its name.

And when it slips from hands so swift,
It rolls away, our daily gift.
In a world of mess, we find delight,
This joyful fruit, our purest rite.

Chasing the Last Ray

Underneath the glowing sky,
We chase the fruit that's flying high.
A spot of orange, bold and bright,
We leap and dash, it's quite a sight!

A cheeky breeze begins to tease,
As yellow orbs roll with such ease.
A friendly duel, who will prevail?
To catch the treat, we can't curtail.

It blunders forth on garden trails,
With giggles, we recount our fails.
The squishy joy upon our tongue,
In this funny chase, we feel so young!

And when the sun dips out of view,
We all agree our fun was true.
With laughter echoing in the dark,
The sweetest prize was a simple spark.

Sweet Drizzle of Tropical Glow

A fruit of laughter, sweet and bright,
Dancing in the warm daylight.
With sticky fingers and silly grins,
We dive right in, let the fun begin!

The juice runs down, a golden stream,
Like silly jokes that burst and beam.
With every bite, a joke's revealed,
In this sweet mess, our joy's unsealed.

A scoff, a giggle, a splash of cheer,
This fruity caper brings us near.
We spin and drop, a silly feat,
Lost in the flavor, dancing on our feet.

So gather round and take a slice,
This sugary comet, oh so nice!
In every drop, the fun won't cease,
With each sweet taste, we find our peace.

Garden of Golden Moments

In a garden where giggles bloom,
Golden wonders sweep the room.
Our laughter echoes through the trees,
As playful fruits dance in the breeze.

We pluck the cheer from branches high,
With every toss, we touch the sky.
A contest born of fruity fate,
With sticky joy, we celebrate!

And every drop that hits the ground,
Turns into giggles all around.
A sunlit patch where fun abounds,
In this funny fruit, our joy resounds.

So join the fray, let spirits soar,
With every bite, we laugh some more.
In this golden garden, take your stand,
And savor life, hand in hand.

A Citrus Labyrinth of Delight

In a twisty grove, I lost my way,
A fruit so bright, it made me stay.
With sticky fingers and a grin,
I danced right in, let the fun begin!

Lemons giggled, oranges flipped,
While I was busy, my pants were ripped.
A parrot squawked, 'Hey, what's the rush?'
I tripped and fell, in a citrus hush!

The scent so sweet, it tickled my nose,
I sneezed and startled a garden hose.
It sprayed like laughter all over me,
In this fruity maze, I'm wild and free!

So here I am, in zest and cheer,
In this labyrinth, there's nothing to fear.
With every step, I slip and glide,
In a citrus dream, where joy won't hide.

Sunkissed Breezes at Twilight

As daylight fades, the breeze takes flight,
Whispers of laughter dance in the night.
Chasing shadows, we jump and prance,
Caught in the rhythm, lost in the chance!

A kite soared high, made of bright hues,
Tangled in branches, it began to muse.
'What a view!' it proudly sighed,
While we yelled, 'Now who's the guide?'

The hammock swung like a boat at sea,
I tried to jump in, but fell on a bee.
It buzzed in laughter, as I rolled away,
Breezy fun turns stings into play!

As stars twinkle, we toast with cheer,
To breezy tales and fruity beer.
With giggles and joy, we bask in delight,
Sunkissed dreams take off into the night!

Timeless Dance of Warmth

Under the glow of the sky's warm smile,
We twirled and twisted, oh what a while!
The ground beneath us, it felt like jelly,
We danced like fools, all goofy and smelly!

The sun winks bright, as we jump and sway,
My friend lost balance and rolled away.
A tumble, a giggle, a splash of drink,
What fun it is, in the sun's hearty wink!

We threw our hats, in a playful jest,
'Catch it if you can!' I yelled with zest.
It soared like a plane, then landed in mud,
Covered in laughter, we rolled in the flood!

With echoes of joy, we waltzed around,
In timeless dance, our spirits unbound.
While warmth embraced us, friends unite,
In this silly moment, all feels just right!

Golden Elixirs of Atmosphere

In a golden cup, happiness flows,
I sipped and swirled, forgot my woes.
The flavors tickled, like giggling friends,
As I clinked my glass, the fun never ends!

'Is that a fruit or a golden crown?'
I asked my buddy, still sipping down.
With one big gulp, I made it disappear,
'Oh wait! Was that parsley?' I shouted in fear!

In the summer glow, every sip's a delight,
We mix up our drinks, tirelessly bright.
With bubbles and laughter, we toast to the sky,
Golden elixirs make us dance high!

Time melts away as we sip and play,
Each drop like sunshine at the end of the day.
With cheeky sips, we cheer for our fate,
In this boozy bliss, we're never late!

The Feast of Warm Days

Oh, what a season, ripe and bright,
Sticky fingers in sunlight's light.
With laughter spilled like juice on the ground,
Chasing the flavor, round and round.

Butterflies giggle, bees dance around,
Nature's buffet is quite profound.
Between the sips of nectar divine,
Who knew a snack could be so fine!

Come gather, my friends, there's plenty to share,
With smiles so big, we won't have a care.
Let's fill our baskets, life is a treat,
Savoring sunshine, oh, isn't it sweet?

The warmth embraces, a whimsical day,
Pitting our laughter in a cheeky way.
As funny as clowns in a fruit-filled spree,
Join in the feast; it's wild and free!

Sun-drenched Joy on Your Palate

A sip of sweetness, quite unlike others,
Laughter and juice, we're all big brothers.
Sunlight drips down, refrain of delight,
Tasting the warmth as day turns to night.

With every bite, joy bursts free,
A sticky affair, just you and me.
Oh, but beware of the drippy plan,
Napkins in hand, we're a slippery clan!

Faces all covered, we chuckle and cheer,
As fruit-flavored giggles fill the warm air.
Every squish is a new witticism,
Where's the next morsel? Our sugary wisdom!

In this sunny banquet, bright as a sprite,
Let's dance with crumbs, what a silly sight!
Cake or pie? We declare: why not all?
With sun-drenched joy, we'll have a ball!

Sweetness Unfurled at Dusk

As dusk approaches, light starts to fade,
With sweet surprises that love has made.
Laughter echoes as the sun says bye,
Under a sky sprinkled with cherry pie.

Frogs start to croak, the rhythm we need,
While we gobble down treats like a steed.
Spoonfuls of giggles and hearty sighs,
Watch our bliss dance beneath purple skies!

Decked out in flavors, a festival feast,
Chasing the sweetness, oh, never ceased.
With our spoon as our compass, let's explore,
For tastes unending, we wish for more!

Each moment we cherish, adorned in joy,
Swirling through tastes like a childish ploy.
With sweetness unfurled, oh what delight,
Endings are only first bites of night!

A Thrill Among the Canopy

In the thick of trees, we plot and plan,
Swinging like monkeys, oh, isn't it grand?
With fruit-filled dreams in our mischievous sights,
We leap for the sweetness, the fun ignites!

A tangle of laughter, we climb and we strive,
Each branch an adventure, oh, feel alive!
Squeezed into joy, it drips from the leaves,
Whispers of berries that everyone believes.

With each reaching grasp, oh, what a thrill,
Dripping with glee, making time stand still.
In our wild canopy, games can't be beat,
Escaping the ground, our hearts skip a beat!

Rolling down hills like a fruity parade,
With the vineyards of giggles so brilliantly laid.
Joy's laughter dances, a song in the air,
In this stunning jungle, forget all your care!

Dances of the Warm Horizon

Beneath the bright and glowing sphere,
Bananas dance, they cheer and jeer.
The coconuts twist, and laughter flies,
While all the fruits join in surprise.

The pineapples roll in haphazard glee,
As watermelons shout, "Look at me!"
Limes are giggling, what a delight,
Under the warm glow of the bright light.

Papayas tumble, oranges sway,
Each one thinking it's their day.
The warm breeze teases, and they agree,
This party's great, just let them be!

With every jiggle, the coconuts grin,
Soon the avocados join in the spin.
As laughter bubbles and fun's the key,
They celebrate joy, just to be free!

Amber Laughs at Dusk

As shadows stretch in playful play,
The night-time fruits come out to sway.
Laughs and giggles fill the air,
With every glow, it's quite the affair.

Twilight twirls, it's quite absurd,
Bananas honk like a silly bird.
Figs are pulling off a funky dance,
While passionfruits steal a quick glance.

In the amber glow, they swirl around,
Each twist and turn makes silly sounds.
Kumquats juggling, trying to stall,
While pineapples inch, not wanting to fall.

The mellow hues bring out their best,
A fruity party, they never rest.
Under the laughter of a dusk so grand,
They shimmy and shake, no plans are planned!

Juicy Whispers in the Breeze

In the garden where the laughter lies,
Fruits exchange their funny ties.
Whispers flutter on the evening breeze,
As cherries chuckle, no need to please.

Lemons laugh with zesty flair,
While bushes tremble, it's quite a scare.
Grapes are giggling, their skins so tight,
While peaches blush in the fading light.

The breeze tells secrets, oh so sweet,
As fruit snacks gather for a cheeky treat.
Kiwis squeal and roll away,
In a juicy game that's here to stay!

Swaying gently with every tease,
Tropics echo with fun-filled ease.
They laugh and chatter, a fruit parade,
Under the stars, their joy won't fade!

Sunkissed Sweetness

A golden glow spills through the trees,
Bringing smiles as sweet as honey breeze.
Mirthful mangos share their delight,
In warm embraces, they shine so bright.

Sunkissed laughter, oh what a treat,
Strawberries bouncing to the beat.
Pineapples jump, their spiky crowns,
As they shake off their silly frowns.

Watermelons roll with playful cheer,
While papayas juggle without fear.
Juicy antics, it's a flavorful mess,
A fruity fest that won't distress!

In this circus of jovial fruit,
No one is shy, they're all astute.
Wrapped in sunlight, their spirits soar,
Here in the sweetness, forevermore!

Golden Promises of Summer

Bright orbs dangle from leafy trees,
Promises of sweetness danced on the breeze.
Squirrels plot heists with cheeky grins,
While ants throw parties with their juicy wins.

A rogue breeze sneaks a fruit's debut,
Rolling right into an unsuspecting shoe.
Juice dribbles down like a laughing child,
Who knew summer could be this wild?

Birds squawk tales of golden delight,
As they swoop and dive, what a sight!
Underneath a sky that's so very blue,
Nature's good humor is built just for you.

When the sun sets on a warm afternoon,
Laughter echoes a playful tune.
Those golden gems hanging like clowns,
Transforming frowns into cheerful crowns.

Heat's Embrace in Orchard Valley

In the orchard where warmth plays tricks,
Fruits hang low, giving gardeners kicks.
Laughter erupts from a sour-faced pear,
While grapes gossip, hanging without a care.

Sweat drips down, combining with glee,
Making us question if ripe fruit's a spree.
A sunburned nose, like a cherry bright,
Tells tales of battles fought in the light.

Around the trees, the shadows conspire,
Plotting escapes from the sun's wild fire.
"Oh look!" yells one, "A daydream escapes!"
And off they go in a dance of capes.

With each juicy bite, the world turns mad,
Crazy beats join this fruity fad.
In orchard valley, where mischief's the law,
Every fruit has a story that leaves us in awe.

Dancing Shadows of Ripened Days

Underneath a tree, the shadows sway,
Telling secrets of a bright, sunny day.
Giggles erupt as the breeze takes a turn,
Whisking away the sun's bubbling burn.

Lemons prank the oranges, calling them lame,
While cherries giggle, playing their game.
"Oh, look at me!" cries a peach that's shy,
"Someone bite me, I promise to fly!"

Laughter ensues with each fruity glide,
As the sun winks, a playful guide.
The fruits join hands, a whimsical dance,
Inviting us all for a joyous chance.

In the ripened days, mischief takes flight,
With nature's laughter shining so bright.
Each juicy jest keeps us all in a cheer,
Celebrating summer, gathering near.

Flicker of Daylight in Lush Green

In the heart of a garden, shadows play,
As sunlight dances in a merry ballet.
Leaves wiggle with joy, feeling the beat,
While hidden critters tap their tiny feet.

A pop here and there, with laughter it sings,
Ripened treasures bring the light that it brings.
Fruits chuckle softly as blossoms conspire,
To create a summer of pure, sweet fire.

Beneath the boughs, there's a party alive,
Where each plump morsel is ready to thrive.
A tickle of zest in every warm breeze,
Makes even the shyest of fruits giggle with ease.

So let the daylight flicker and gleam,
With nature's antics, join in the dream.
In lush green corners, fun never ends,
Summer's mischief is where laughter blends.

Gleaming Spheres of Delight

In a bowl of fruit, they play,
With a shiny grin, bright as day.
They tease the tongue, they wink and sway,
Oh, what a tangy, joyful way!

Squeezed too hard, it's juice galore,
Splattering friends, they beg for more.
A fruit fight breaks out, such a chore,
But laughter echoes, who could ignore?

Their golden hue brings silly smiles,
Every bite's worth our wild trials.
Dancing winds and fruity styles,
Who knew fruit could spark such wiles?

So gather round, let's make a toast,
To juicy spheres we love the most.
In every laugh, in every boast,
These silly treats are what we coast!

Warmth Wrapped in Juices

A sweet surprise in every slice,
Messy faces, oh, isn't it nice?
Sticky hands, roll the dice,
Each drop lands like a sugary spice.

Sunshine drips on every plate,
Taste buds sing, we celebrate.
Juicy hugs while we await,
The fruit parade, isn't it great?

With every squeeze, we share a look,
Dessert's a laugh, not just a book.
Eating faster than we cook,
In fruity chaos, we are hooked!

Even the ants join in the fun,
Dancing 'round till the day is done.
With every bite, we've just begun,
Juicy joy for everyone!

Twilight's Fruity Embrace

In the evening glow, they gleam,
With a flavor that's a sweet dream.
They sway and giggle, or so it seems,
Caught up in our twilight schemes.

We cut them open, laughter bursts,
With every scoop, our joy rehearsed.
From smoothies to pies, we'll quench our thirst,
In fruity chaos, we're well-versed.

Sneaky peeks at who'll take the last,
In this fruity race, it goes so fast.
Each splash and squirt, a delicious blast,
A party in our hands, unsurpassed!

With every taste, the night ignites,
Bold flavors dancing, what a sight!
As laughter fills the starry heights,
We feast on joy and silly bites!

Citrus Reverie

When dawn arrives, they wink awake,
Juicy slices for the day we make.
Sour smiles and giggles break,
Each zesty bite a playful quake.

On breakfast plates, like stars they shine,
With fruity jokes, we drink the brine.
A citrus splash, oh how divine,
A punchline wrapped in every rind!

They hide in salads, they tease the eye,
In every mix, they catch you by.
With every seed, a chuckle, oh my!
These playful treasures, how they fly!

So squeeze them tight, unleash the cheer,
In joyful bites, we draw them near.
With laughs and juice, the path is clear,
Delightful chaos, let's hold dear!

A Serenade of Sunlit Orchards

In orchards bright where sweetness grows,
The fruit hangs low, in funny rows.
A squirrel dashes, takes a bite,
Then scurries off, what a sight!

The shadows dance beneath the trees,
As bees buzz by with utmost ease.
A merry tune begins to play,
While ripe delights come out to play!

Each plump delight a playful tease,
With sticky fingers, oh, what a breeze!
We laugh and munch from dawn till dusk,
In fruity bliss, it's quite robust!

A world of fun, this orchard land,
With treasures ripe and laughter planned.
So take a bite, and join the cheer,
For sunny days are often near!

Radiant Tropic Whispers

In tropic dreams where laughter sways,
The leafy dance of sunlit rays.
A parrot squawks, a playful tease,
While monkeys swing with perfect ease!

When fruit drops down with playful thuds,
We dodge and dive, amidst the floods.
Each giggle bursts, a zesty thrill,
As friends unite for endless fill!

A splash of juice, a playful fight,
Makes every day a pure delight.
In radiant shades of green and gold,
These sunny tales are sweetly bold!

A toast to joy and fruity zest,
In vibrant dreams, we are the best.
So chipper hearts just swell and soar,
In whispered winds, we laugh for more!

Amber Fruit on a Distant Shore

On distant shores where laughter rings,
Golden fruit does wondrous things.
The tide rolls in, the laughter swells,
As sandy toes find fruity spells!

A playful breeze, a splashy game,
Emerging rays, no two the same.
The seagulls squawk, they join the fun,
While golden treats shine in the sun!

Like little suns, they roll and dance,
With silly ways that leave no chance.
A juicy bite, a squirt, a laugh,
We share the joy, fun's epitaph!

So here's to shores of endless cheer,
With friends around and nothing to fear.
This amber world spins in delight,
As laughter lingers, pure and bright!

Warmth That Lingers in the Breeze

The warmth that tickles, brings a grin,
As fruity joys come rolling in.
A bouncy laugh, a cheerful sound,
As playful gusts swirl all around!

With every bite, a giggly cheer,
As juices splash, we hold them dear.
A fruit-filled day, no cares in sight,
With tasty smiles, it feels just right!

We chase the rays, we leap and play,
In sunny gardens, come what may.
The world's a stage of fruity prance,
As laughter leads the merry dance!

So let's embrace this joyful breeze,
With whimsical grins and sunlit pleas.
In warmth that lingers, life's a tease,
With fruity fun that's sure to please!

Twilight's Last Glimmer

In the sky, a yellow ball,
Frogs performing a sunny sprawl,
Chasing shadows with a grin,
Every tail out, let the fun begin!

Lemons laugh, wearing bright hues,
Pineapples twist in silly shoes,
Bananas slip on coconut paths,
While monkeys giggle at their own math!

As day fades with a cheeky wink,
Crickets join in, they love to stink,
Squirrels dance in a crazy cheer,
Under the eye of the glowing sphere!

With a splash from a playful wave,
Fish flip over, a party rave,
That twilight glow is hard to beat,
As nature joins in, all on its feet!

A Tropical Ballet of Radiance

In the corner of this paradise,
Dancing leaves all whirl and slice,
Coconuts waltz with graceful ease,
While crabs shuffle, aiming to please!

The breeze, it tickles all around,
As bubbly laughter's the only sound,
Twirling vines in a leafy dress,
A party here is no less than a mess!

Fluttering birds, a colorful crew,
Humming tunes that might make you rue,
Daring to challenge, they dive and pop,
Landing in puddles, a glittering plop!

Even the ants have caught the beat,
Marching in line, oh, what a feat,
Gathering crumbs with a tap-tap sound,
In this jolly dance, joy can be found!

The Sweetness of Golden Skies

Golden blobs in a melting dream,
Fruits planning a vibrant scheme,
Winking clouds on a lazy ride,
While giggling heights play peek and hide!

Laughter drips from the tallest trees,
Tickling time like a gentle breeze,
Pineapple kings on juicy thrones,
As playful breezes steal their cones!

Watermelon floats, oh what a sight,
Bouncing around, pure delight,
Fruit bats swoop, or so they say,
Making a splash in the sunny bay!

With every blush of the twilight hue,
Nature's show takes a bow, it's true,
A funny finish, a drop of grace,
As daylight dances, leaving its trace!

A Playground of Lush Light

In the shade where the giggles play,
Under the watch of a palmy sway,
Bouncing berries in a jolly race,
While sunshine paints a happy face!

Mangoes juggling like they're on stage,
With a plume of feathers, what a rage,
Laughs burst out like pops from a can,
As toucans strut with a game plan!

Coconuts roll with a silly thud,
Creating a game of fruit and mud,
Chasing shadows, trying to score,
In this fun land, who could ask for more?

Even the clouds peek down in surprise,
At playful antics that light up the skies,
With each twirl and each grunt of glee,
This playground thrives, wild and free!

www.ingramcontent.com/pod-product-compliance
Ingram Content Group UK Ltd.
Pitfield, Milton Keynes, MK11 3LW, UK
UKHW021001100325
4924UKWH00032B/313